Draw Your
P E T !

You Can Draw

Birds!

Katie Dicker

Gareth Stevens
Publishing

Please visit our website, www.garethstevens.com. For a free color catalog of all our high-quality books, call toll free 1-800-542-2595 or fax 1-877-542-2596.

Library of Congress Cataloging-in-Publication Data

Dicker, Katie.
 You can draw birds! / Katie Dicker.
     pages cm. — (Draw your pet!)
 Includes index.
ISBN 978-1-4339-8724-3 (pbk.)
ISBN 978-1-4339-8725-0 (6-pack)
ISBN 978-1-4339-8723-6 (library binding)
1. Birds in art—Juvenile literature. 2. Drawing—Technique—Juvenile literature. I. Title.
 NC782.D53 2013
 743.6'8—dc23

                              2012033133

Published in 2013 by
Gareth Stevens Publishing
111 East 14th Street, Suite 349
New York, NY 10003

© 2013 Gareth Stevens Publishing

Produced for Gareth Stevens by Calcium Creative Ltd
Illustrated by Mike Lacey
Designed by Paul Myerscough
Edited by Sarah Eason and Harriet McGregor

Photo credits: Shutterstock: Valery Bareta 4, 10t, Andrew Bignell 26t, Katrina Brown 10b, Bryoni Castelijn 20b, Mikael Damkier 18t, Pichugin Dmitry 22t, Anna Hoychuk 6l, Eric Isselée cover, 14l, 14r, 16, 22b, 26b, Jagodka 6r, Marina Jay 24, 28, Sara Robinson 12, Susan Schmitz 18, VitCOM Photo 8.

Printed in the United States of America

CPSIA compliance information: Batch CW13GS: For further information contact Gareth Stevens, New York, New York at 1-800-542-2595.

Contents

You Can Draw Birds!

If you love birds, you'll love to draw them, too! Birds are supersmart creatures that have lived on Earth for thousands of years. They make lively and fun pets, and are beautiful to watch.

There are many different types of bird. Many people choose to keep tropical birds because they have beautiful colors and markings and love to talk with their owners. Every type of bird has special needs. Some birds, such as budgerigars, can live happily in a small cage. Other birds, such as African grays, need larger areas. In this book, we'll teach you how to care for birds—and how to draw them, too.

Discover how to draw birds!

Follow the steps that show you how to draw each type of bird. Then draw from a photograph of your own pet to create a special pet portrait!

You Will Need:

- Art paper and pencils
- Eraser
- Coloring pens and/or paints and a paintbrush

parakeets

cockatiels

budgerigars

canaries

African grays

lovebirds

Budgerigars

Budgerigars are also known as budgies and the common parakeet. These small, colorful birds can be kept indoors in a cage or outside in an aviary in warm weather. Budgies can live for up to 15 years.

Budgies come in lots of different colors, including blue, green, and yellow.

 **Step**

First, draw the bird's outline. Have your bird standing on a straight wooden pole. As you draw, carefully check the proportions of the bird's body, such as the distance from the head to the feet.

 **Step**

Now add some detailed lines to your picture. First, pencil the outline of the bird's feet. Be sure to draw the claws on the feet with a steady hand.

 **Step**

Lightly pencil the features of the bird's face to show the eye and the beak. Then go over the features with a heavier pencil line.

Caring for your budgie

- It is best to keep two or three budgies. They are friendly animals that do not like to live alone.

- Make sure you include a birdbath in your budgie's cage. These birds love to bathe.

- Put toys, such as mirrors and balls, inside your pet's cage. Budgies are smart, active birds that need plenty of toys to play with.

Budgies use their long, clawed feet to hold on to twigs and the fingers of their owner.

Step

Draw lots of fine pencil lines to add the detail of the budgie's feathers. Draw some claws on the bird's feet. Then shade parts of the bird's head, neck, body, and feet to add depth. Don't forget to shade the pole, too!

Step

Now you can finish your picture by adding color. Use a light blue for the body and white for the head and tail. Add depth using darker shades. Then color the beak yellow and the eye black. Use a brown color for the wooden pole.

Cockatiels

The pretty, colorful cockatiel loves company! They are best kept in pairs or large groups of cockatiels. Cockatiels are very curious and smart. They love to climb and jump around their cage, and will peek into every corner!

Cockatiels have a large "quiff" of feathers on their heads.

Step

Draw the outline for your bird. Can you see how it is looking around, with the quiff on its head raised high? Draw the bird's feet on the ground, and the tail slightly lifted.

Step

Pencil the beak and the shape of the wings. Draw the outline of the bird's belly.

Step

Now draw your bird's eye. Add light shading strokes to the head, wings, and tail to show some of the feathery detail.

Caring for your cockatiel

- These active birds need regular exercise, so they are happy living in an aviary. If you keep your bird indoors, be sure you let it fly outside of the cage, too.

- Your cockatiel will love eating small pieces of fruit as treats. Be sure not to give your bird anything other than seeds, fruit, and water—other foods or liquids can make it sick.

- Talk to your cockatiel, and it will talk to you! These birds are amazing mimics and will easily pick up words. Be careful what you say!

Give your pet plenty of toys to play with. Cockatiels love to play games.

Step

Add more detail to the bird's body. Draw the splotch on its face. Give the wings, neck, and tail some more feathers, and add the claws on the feet.

Step 5

Now bring your bird to life with some color! Choose a palette of gray, white, and black for the body, and a light yellow for the head. Add an orange-red splotch to the face. Finally, add some shading around the eye socket and beneath the tail and belly to give your picture depth.

Canaries

Canaries are a lot of fun to care for. These birds love to talk with their owner and are easy to keep. Canaries come from Africa and can live for up to 10 years as pets.

Canaries come in lots of different colors including orange, brown, white, or yellow.

Step 1

Draw the outline of your bird. Show the angle of the tilted head and the left foot gripping a wooden branch. Don't forget to include the outline of the canary's tail feathers, too.

Step 2

Pencil the outline of the bird's right leg and foot, and add detail to its claws. Draw each foot tightly wrapped around the wooden branch beneath.

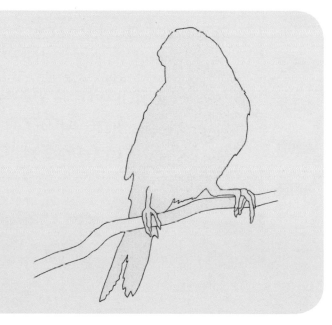

Step 3

Now add some detail to the bird's face. Draw one of its beady eyes, and pencil the outline of the beak. Notice how the eye is on the side of the face.

Caring for your canary

- Keep your canary in a cage indoors, or an aviary outside. These birds need to fly a lot of the time. If you keep your pet in an indoor cage, be sure to let it fly around your home from time to time.

- At night, cover your pet's cage with a sheet or blanket to help it sleep. Canaries get up as soon as it is light and may be quite noisy. To keep your pet quiet first thing in the morning, keep its cage dark!

- Be careful when you pick up your bird. Canaries can become jumpy and frightened if handled roughly. Try to be kind and gentle with your pet.

Canaries love to be around other birds. Try to keep more than one canary as a pet.

Step

Use lots of fine pencil strokes to add shading and depth to your picture. Show the feathery body, wings, and tail. Then add lines to the wooden branch.

Step 5

Now show off your canary with some color! Use a pretty, bright red for the feathers. Use darker shades to show the roundness of the bird's belly. Use a palette of pink or gray for the beak and feet, and a rich brown for the branch. Finally, use a white tint to put a twinkle in your feathered friend's eye!

African Grays

These birds are beautiful, gray-colored parrots. They are one of the most friendly of parrots and love to be around their owner. African grays make such great pets that they have been kept by people for 4,000 years.

Drawings of African gray parrots as pets can be seen in Egyptian hieroglyphs!

Draw your African gray from the side. You can add the rough lines of the legs and feet at this stage. Show the outline of the bird's sharp claws, too.

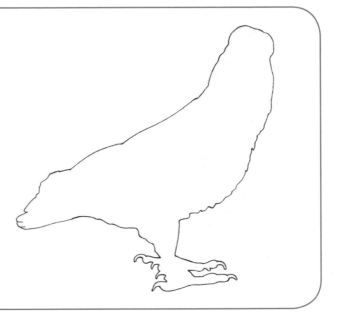

Step

Now add the outline of the bird's wing and tail feathers. Add more detail to the claws and draw the bird's foot ring. This ring has information about the bird and where it comes from in case it ever gets lost.

Step

Now focus on the bird's face. Add two beady eyes on each side and show the detail of the beak. Begin to add more tail feathers, too.

Caring for your African gray

- Don't choose a round cage—it may make your bird confused. A square or rectangular cage is best.

- Be sure to keep your bird in a large cage. It should be at least 4 feet (122 cm) tall. African grays need plenty of space in which to move around.

- Along with a seed diet, you can also give your bird spinach and curly kale. Parrots love their greens!

- Talk to your parrot often. These birds need a lot of attention to stop them from becoming bored.

African gray babies are covered in lots of soft gray and white feathers.

Add lots of fine lines to the
bird's body to show the soft
feathers on its neck, chest,
and wings. Use heavier and
lighter pencil strokes to show
the different types of feathers
that cover the African gray.

Step 5

Color your drawing using a palette
of black, white, and gray. These
different shades will also give
your picture more depth. Include
a bright splotch of pink on the
feathers of the bird's tail and leg.

Lovebirds

The smallest and cutest of all parrots is the lovebird. These pretty little birds come in lots of different colors, from orange and green to pink and blue. Lovebirds are active parrots and can be very noisy!

Like many tropical parrots, lovebirds love to be around lots of other birds.

Step 1

First, draw the outline of your lovebird. Draw the bird from the side. Pencil the hooked beak and the bird's long feet and claws.

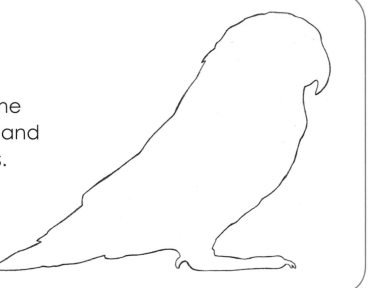

Step 2

Now add more detail to the beak. Draw the sharp claws (notice how this parrot has a hind claw), and include the foot ring. Pencil the outline of the bird's wing, too.

Step 3

Draw an eye on the side of the lovebird's head, and give it a wide rim. Then add more detail to the wing feathers.

Caring for your lovebird

- Give your pet little pieces of fruit as a treat. Its main diet should be made up of seeds.

- Make sure your bird's cage has lots of toys. Lovebirds are very active and smart.

- Be patient while taming your new lovebird pet. It is best to buy a lovebird under four months old. That way the baby bird can bond with you as its protector, just like it would with its parent.

These colorful birds are gorgeous to look at.

Step

With a fine-tipped pencil, add some texture to the parrot's feathers. Be sure to use small strokes. Fill in the detail of the beady eye, and its sharp beak. Then focus on the legs, feet, and claws.

Step 5

Finish your picture by coloring it. Use a palette of colorful shades to bring your lovebird to life. Pick a rich green for the wings, with lighter shades for the legs and belly. Choose an orange for the head, pink for the beak, and white for the tip of the tail feathers. Add a white rim around the eye, too. Finally, use a white tint on your lovebird's eye.

Parakeets

Parakeets are small- to medium-sized parrots with very long tail feathers. They measure around 7 to 10 inches (17.8 to 25.4 cm) from the top of their heads to the end of their tails.

Parakeets have lots of crazy-colored, fluffy feathers!

Step 1

Draw your parakeet facing you, with its head slightly tilted to one side. Include the detail of the sharp beak, the tail, and the two feet with claws.

Step 2

Pencil the outline of the parrot's legs, and add some detail to its beak. Note how long the tail is in proportion to the bird's legs and body.

Step 3

Pencil the features of your parakeet's face. Draw its beady eye, and add a nostril above its beak.

Caring for your parakeet

- Choose a large cage for your pet. Parakeets are on the move almost all of the time, and love to climb and explore their space.

- Talk to your bird—parakeets can mimic lots of words and love the attention of their owner.

- This bird loves to have fun! You will need to keep it happy with lots of toys. Parakeets love to play with objects such as empty coconut shells and seashells. You can also buy fun bird toys from pet stores.

Some parakeets can live for up to 70 years.

Step

Use a fine-tipped pencil to add some texture to the bird's body. Use fine strokes to show the soft feathers of its neck and belly, and try longer strokes for the tail feathers.

Step 5

Complete your picture by adding some color. Use a palette of bright shades including reds, greens, yellows, and blues. Use a different color for the bird's iris, and the feathers around the eye. Finally, use a light gray for the parakeet's sharp claws.

Glossary

active: moving

attention: to focus on something

aviary: a large outdoor cage in which birds are kept

beady: like a bead

bond: to feel close to an animal or a person

confused: dizzy, unable to understand what is happening

curious: wanting to find out about things

curly kale: a dark green leafy vegetable

detail: the fine pencil markings on a drawing

explore: to discover more about a place

eye socket: the hollow in the head in which the eyeball sits

foot ring: a metal ring used to show where a bird comes from

hieroglyphs: ancient Egyptian writing made up of pictures

iris: the colored part of an eye

markings: the patterns on an animal's fur or feathers

mimic: an animal that can copy sounds or behaviors of people or other animals. Also, to copy.

nostril: the opening through which something breathes

palette: a range of colors

proportion: the size of one part of the body in relation to another

protector: a person who looks after something or someone

quiff: feathers or hair that stands upright on the head

seed: a small part of a plant that contains lots of nutrients that birds need for good health

shade: to use pencil strokes that add depth to a picture

spinach: a dark green leafy vegetable

tame: to stop an animal from behaving in a wild way

tropical: comes from the tropics, parts of the world that are near the equator, an imaginary line around Earth's middle

For More Information

Books

Green, John. *How to Draw Birds*. Mineola, NY: Dover Publications, 1998.

Jeffrey, Laura S. *Birds: How to Choose and Care for a Bird*. American Humane Pet Care Library. Berkeley Heights, NJ: Enslow Elementary, 2004.

Sexton, Brenda. *You Can Draw Pets*. Mankato, MN: Picture Window Books, 2011.

Websites

Find out more about pet birds at:
www.parrotchronicles.com

Discover more about how to look after your pet bird at:
www.birdsnways.com

Index